LIFE IN HOT WATER

T0182719

To my grandchildren, Filomène and Tatum,
who are already exploring their worlds
—M. B.

A special thanks to all scientists, and to authors like
Mary Batten, who strive constantly to bring to light
the wonders that thrive in the deepest parts of our
planet. This book taught me many things.

And as always, I'm grateful to my wife Noni
and my daughter Nina for keeping me excited
about life and its meaning.
—T. G.

Published by
PEACHTREE PUBLISHING COMPANY INC.
1700 Chattahoochee Avenue
Atlanta, Georgia 30318-2112
PeachtreeBooks.com

Text © 2022 by Mary Batten
Illustrations © 2022 by Thomas Gonzalez

First trade paperback edition published in 2024

Edited by Vicky Holifield
Design and composition by Adela Pons

Illustrations created in pastel, colored pencils, and airbrush

Printed and bound in March 2024 by C&C Offset,
Shenzhen, China.
10 9 8 7 6 5 4 3 2 1 (hardcover)
10 9 8 7 6 5 4 3 2 1 (trade paperback)
HC ISBN 978-1-68263-152-2
PB ISBN 978-1-68263-721-0

Cataloging-in-Publication Data is available from the Library of
Congress.

LIFE IN HOT WATER

Wildlife at the Bottom of the Ocean

Written by **Mary Batten**

Illustrated by **Thomas Gonzalez**

PEACHTREE

ATLANTA

In the inky blackness at the bottom of the sea,
where the sun never shines, where water hot enough
to melt lead gushes from chimneys, lie the most
extreme environments on Earth—

hydrothermal vents.

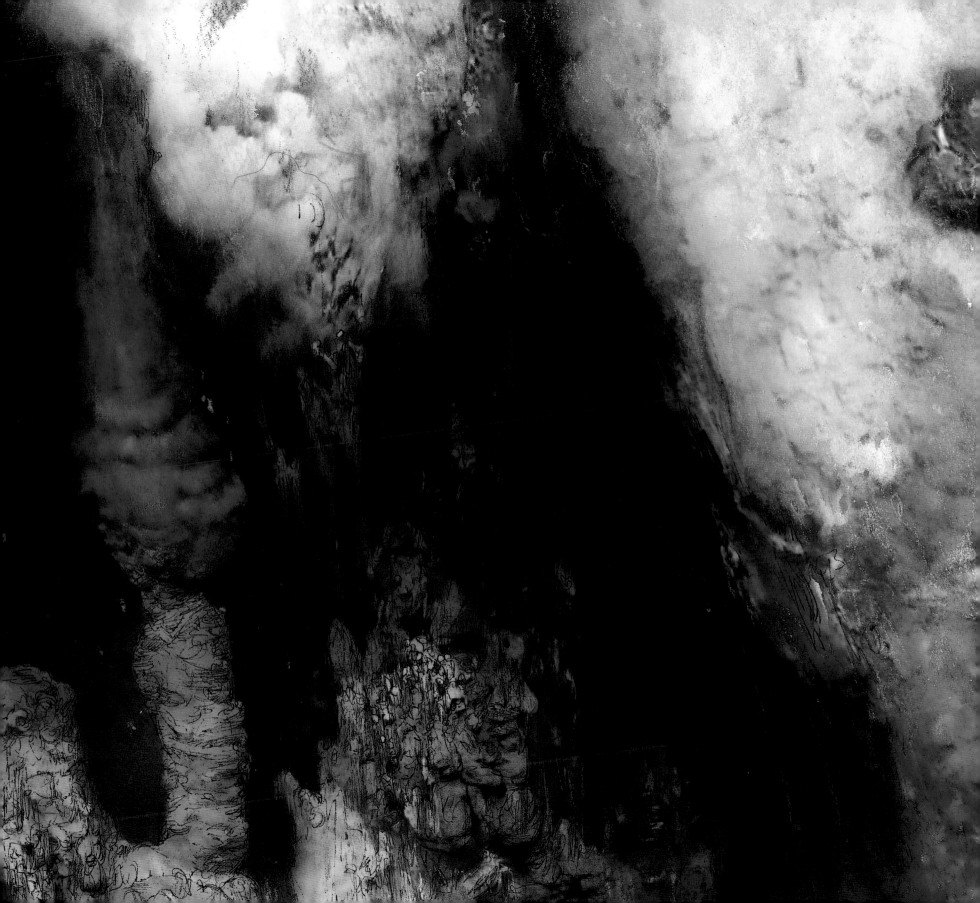

This is a world where liquid Earth and solid Earth interact, where volcanoes erupt daily, gushing plumes of superhot fluids above the seafloor.

You might think nothing could live in this scalding-hot world miles beneath the ocean's surface. But an amazing ecosystem thrives here—one seen no place else on Earth.

Discovering it is one of the greatest adventures in science.

For years geologists had predicted
hydrothermal vents should exist in the deep
ocean, but there was no evidence to support
their prediction. In the early 1970s, the
National Science Foundation funded several
ocean expeditions using remotely operated
vehicles (ROVs) to look for vents. Towing deep-
sea cameras and temperature sensors, these
expeditions identified an area of the mid-ocean
ridge near the Galápagos Islands as a likely
place to find hydrothermal vents.

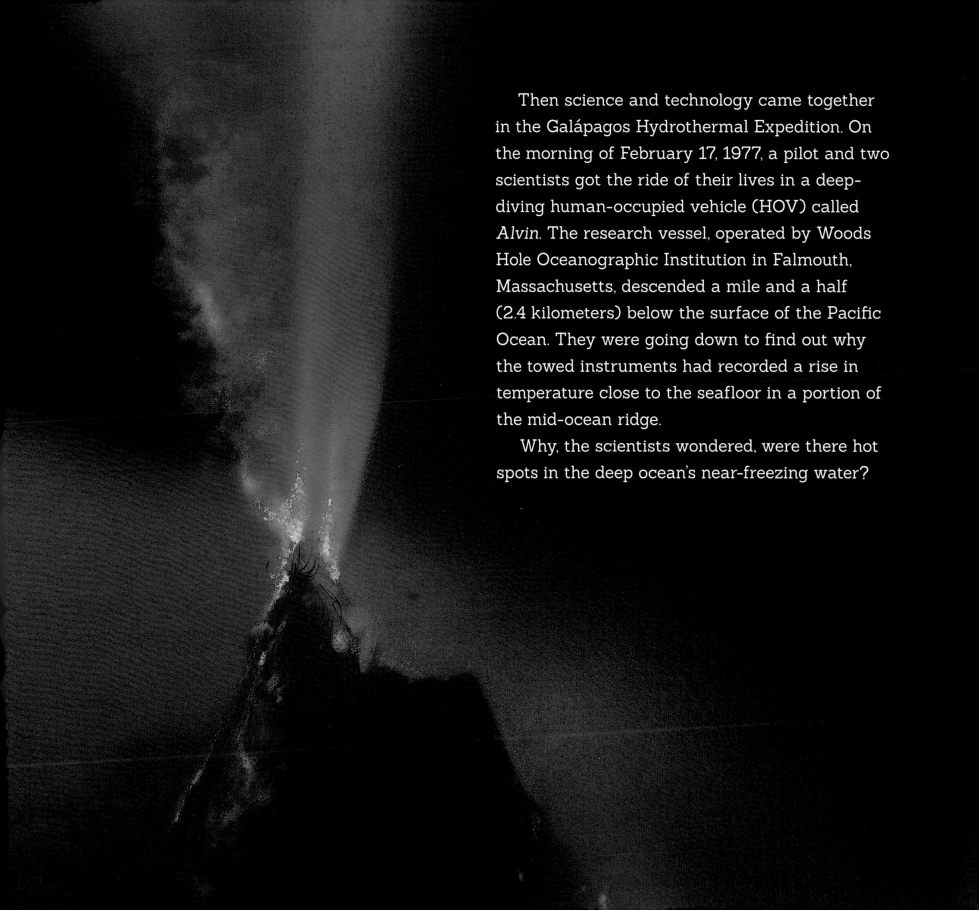

Then science and technology came together in the Galápagos Hydrothermal Expedition. On the morning of February 17, 1977, a pilot and two scientists got the ride of their lives in a deep-diving human-occupied vehicle (HOV) called *Alvin*. The research vessel, operated by Woods Hole Oceanographic Institution in Falmouth, Massachusetts, descended a mile and a half (2.4 kilometers) below the surface of the Pacific Ocean. They were going down to find out why the towed instruments had recorded a rise in temperature close to the seafloor in a portion of the mid-ocean ridge.

Why, the scientists wondered, were there hot spots in the deep ocean's near-freezing water?

Down . . .

　　　down . . .

　　　　down . . .

Alvin descended through the darkness.
When it reached the bottom, the scientists
turned on the lights and looked through
the small portholes. What they saw
was beyond anything they imagined.
Jets of hot, dark-colored fluid were
exploding upward like geysers. In that
breathtaking moment of discovery, the
scientists knew they were the first
human beings to see a hydrothermal
vent, evidence that the geologists'
prediction was accurate.

　　But that wasn't all. Living
creatures, never seen before,
clustered on the rock structures
around the vent. Life where no life
was thought possible.

　　Hydrothermal vents not only
existed; they harbored an entire
ecosystem.

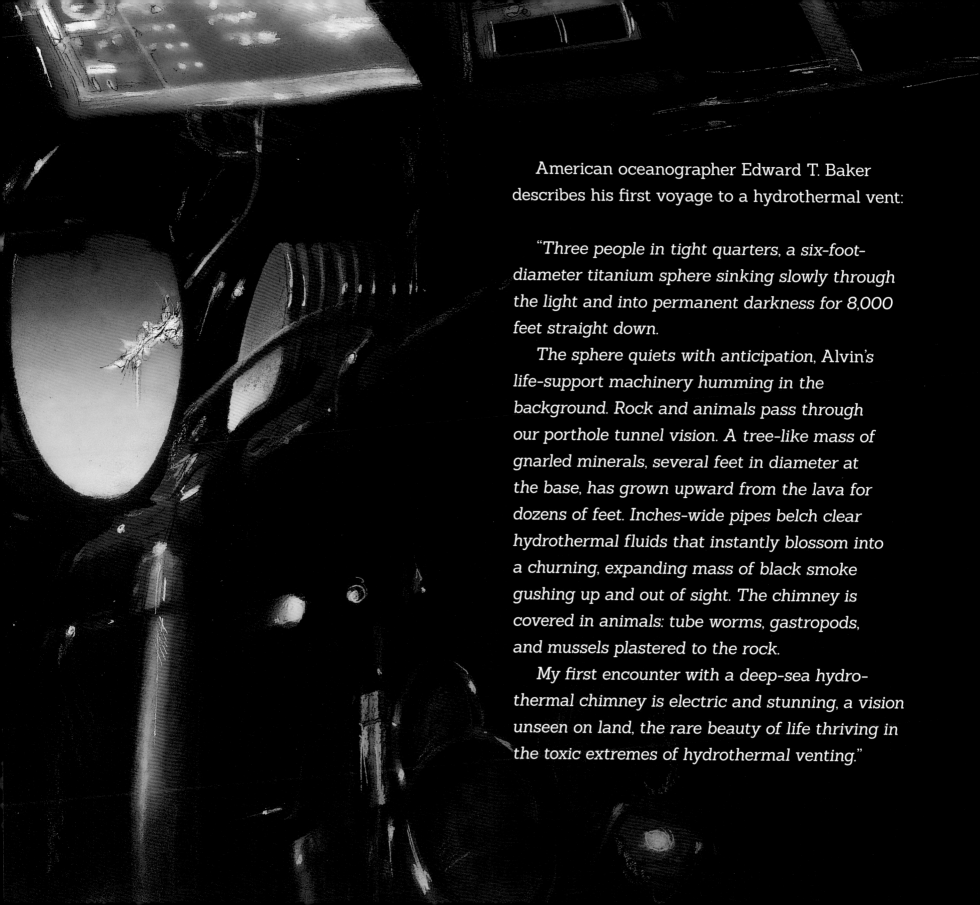

American oceanographer Edward T. Baker describes his first voyage to a hydrothermal vent:

"Three people in tight quarters, a six-foot-diameter titanium sphere sinking slowly through the light and into permanent darkness for 8,000 feet straight down.

The sphere quiets with anticipation, Alvin's life-support machinery humming in the background. Rock and animals pass through our porthole tunnel vision. A tree-like mass of gnarled minerals, several feet in diameter at the base, has grown upward from the lava for dozens of feet. Inches-wide pipes belch clear hydrothermal fluids that instantly blossom into a churning, expanding mass of black smoke gushing up and out of sight. The chimney is covered in animals: tube worms, gastropods, and mussels plastered to the rock.

My first encounter with a deep-sea hydrothermal chimney is electric and stunning, a vision unseen on land, the rare beauty of life thriving in the toxic extremes of hydrothermal venting."

"There's so much about the deep sea that we haven't even begun to explore. It's all discovery, and that makes it exciting."

—Dr. Janet Voight
Associate Curator
Negaunee Integrative Research Center
Field Museum, Chicago, Illinois

CAYMAN TROUGH

MID-ATLANTIC RIDGE

GALÁPAGOS RIDGE

EAST PACIFIC RISE

CHILE RIDGE

PACIFIC-ANTARCTIC RIDGE

Approximate locations of some of the mid-ocean ridges

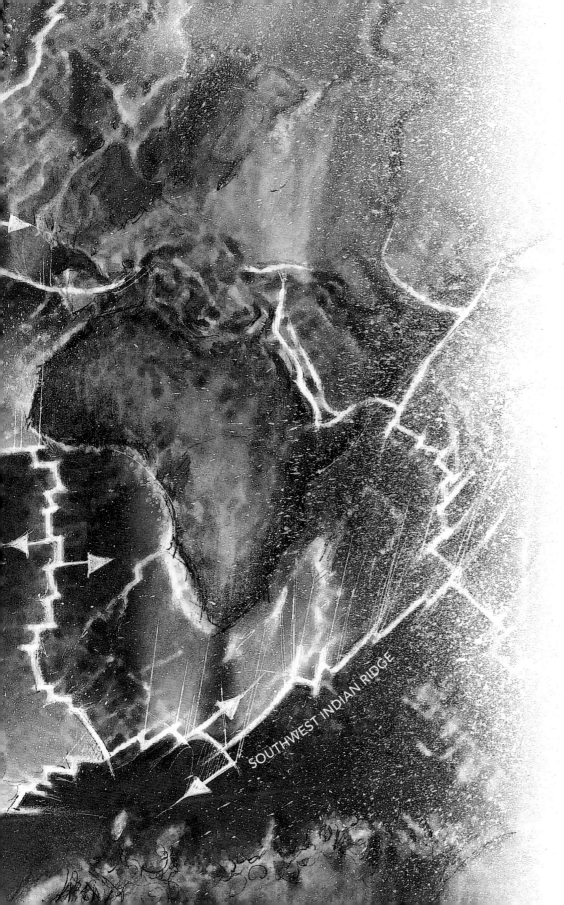

SOUTHWEST INDIAN RIDGE

Hydrothermal vents are underwater hot springs that form along the mid-ocean ridge, the longest mountain range on Earth. You can't see it because it's at the bottom of the sea. There it snakes more than 40,000 miles (65,000 kilometers) around the planet. On the map it looks like the stitching on a baseball. Portions of the ridge lie in each ocean. Underwater volcanoes along the ridge erupt continually, spewing out magma and creating new seafloor.

Over some three billion years, this constant rebuilding of the ocean floor has moved Earth's gigantic crustal plates, called tectonic plates, around like pieces of a puzzle, sometimes separating continents.

Many scientific expeditions have studied the mid-ocean ridges, but only a tiny fraction of them have been explored.

Since that astounding 1977 voyage of discovery in the *Alvin*, researchers have learned much more about hydrothermal vents and how they form.

Volcanoes erupt almost daily along the mid-ocean ridge. These eruptions open cracks in Earth's crust, allowing frigid seawater to seep deep down, where it is heated as high as 752 degrees F (400 degrees C) by magma from inside the Earth. As the seawater heats, it reacts with rocks in the planet's crust, flushing up chemicals and dissolved metals such as copper, gold, and zinc. Jets of hot liquid then burst upward toward the seabed and spew out of the vents in great superhot plumes.

Hydrothermal vents are not all alike. Two types—black smokers and white smokers—gush their hot chemical brew. Of course, it's not real smoke, but the plumes of fluid they give off look like smoke.

When the hot plume contacts the near-freezing seawater, minerals in the fluid crystallize, forming chimneys and spires that tower as much as 80 feet (25 meters) above the seafloor— sometimes more. Scientists named one of the tallest chimneys Godzilla. It reached a height of 150 feet (45 meters) before it toppled over.

White smokers are cooler and spurt a mix of lighter chemicals such as calcium and silicon.

The fluid flowing from black smokers contains iron and sulfide. This gives the plumes a dark color.

The scientists who discovered hydrothermal vents expected to find a barren, rocky seascape. They were so sure that nothing could live there that they had not even included a biologist on the expedition team.

But exploration is often full of surprises. The scientists were astounded when they saw unknown creatures living at the vents. Life was thriving not only in extreme heat and under enormous ocean pressure, but also in complete darkness.

How was it possible?

Until deep-sea vents were discovered, scientists thought all complex ecosystems depended on the sun and green plants. They thought that photosynthesis—the process by which green plants use sunlight to make food—was the base of all food chains. But here they found life without sunlight, without green plants.

What was providing food for animals in this incredibly harsh environment?

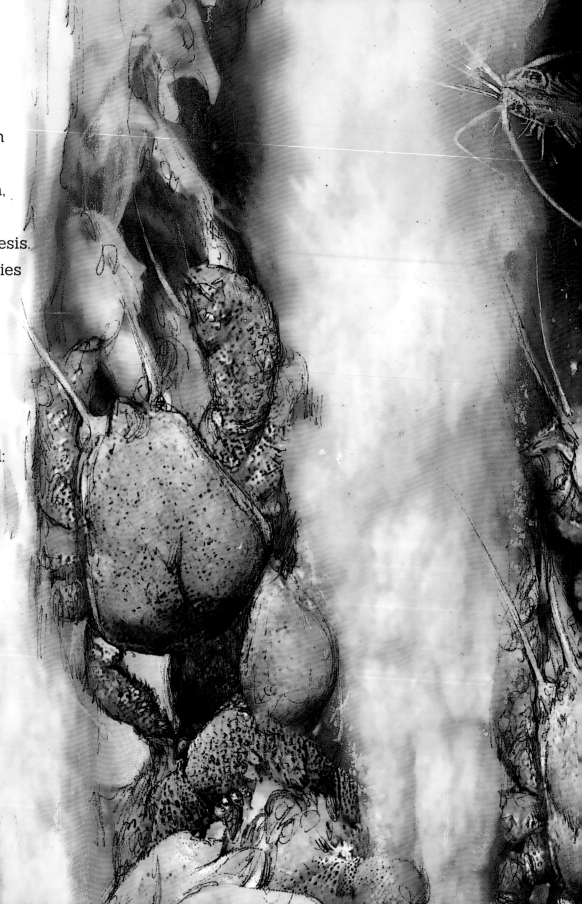

The answer seems like something
out of science fiction. Toxic chemicals in
the vent fluid are the base of vent food
chains. Chemicals from inside the Earth,
not sunlight, power the vent ecosystem.
Scientists call this process chemosynthesis.
It is one of the most important discoveries
of the twentieth century.

This discovery totally changed the
way people think about the conditions
for life. Textbooks had to be rewritten
to include two kinds of food production:
photosynthesis and chemosynthesis.
But another puzzling question remained:

What could eat toxic chemicals?

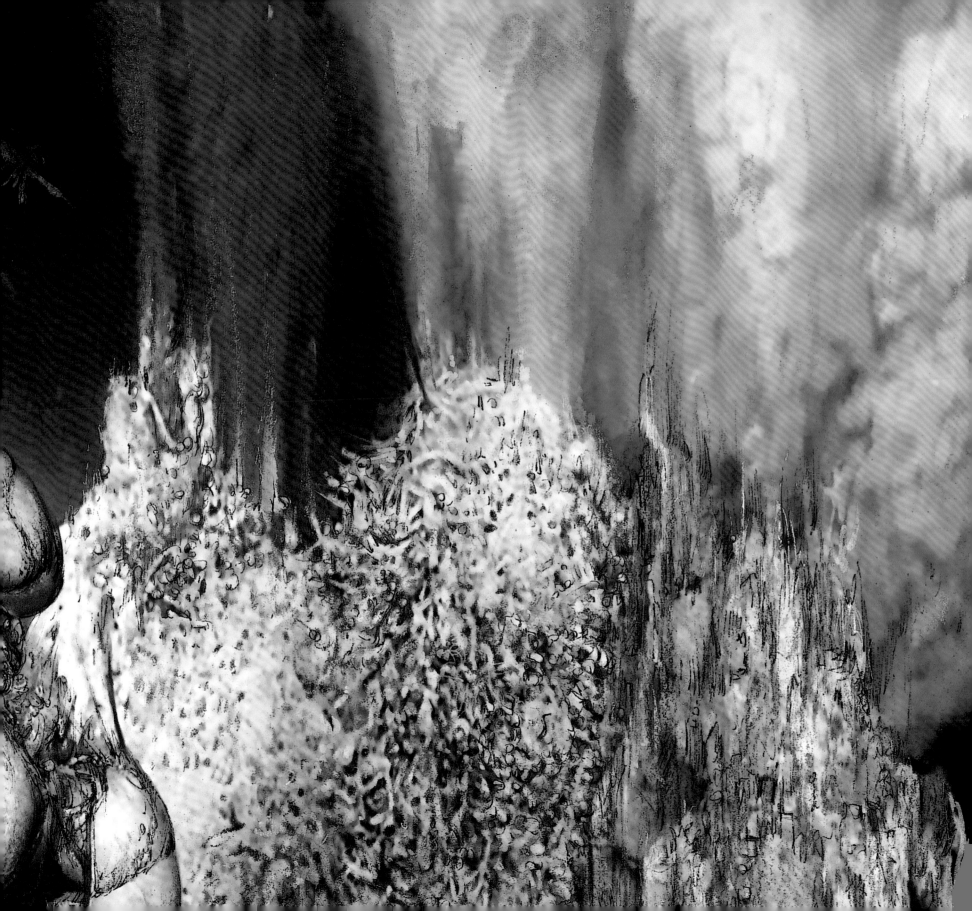

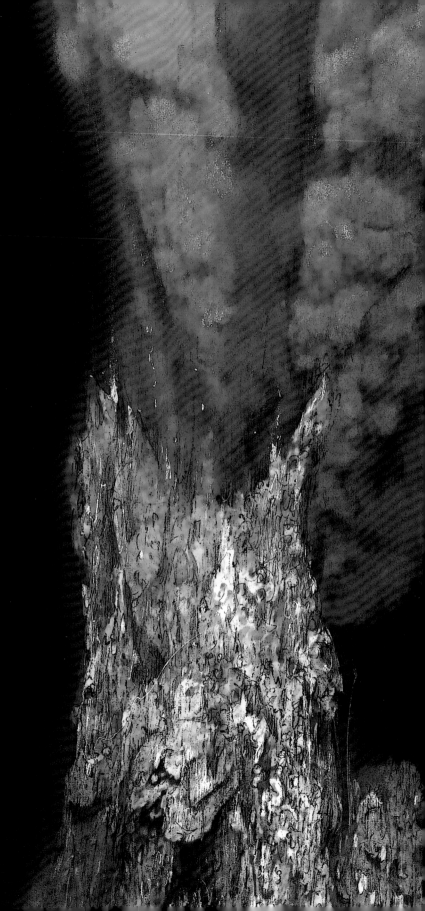

Again, the answer was startling.

Microbes—microscopic organisms.

Billions of bacteria and other microbes eat the poisonous vent chemicals, most notably hydrogen sulfide, the stinky chemical that smells like rotten eggs. The microbes use the chemicals to produce simple sugars on which vent creatures depend. Some vent bacteria live freely in the water. Others live in the bodies of vent animals in a mutually beneficial partnership called symbiosis.

Many vent bacteria can live in higher temperatures (235 degrees F /113 degrees C) than any other organism on the planet.

Scientists call organisms that can tolerate such extreme conditions extremophiles.

"Volcanoes plus water equals life."

—Dr. Edward T. Baker
Earth-Ocean Interactions
NOAA/Pacific Marine
Environmental Laboratory, U.S.

Over 900 new species of vent animals are known, and more may be discovered as exploration continues.

One of the most amazing is the scaly-foot snail that lives on black smoker vent chimneys in the Indian Ocean. You can think of it as the "iron snail" because it is the only animal that has an iron shell. Hundreds of iron scales cover its foot. The iron comes from vent fluids.

The snail has its own energy supply from bacteria living inside a special gland in its body. While its armor helps protect it from predators, the scaly-foot snail now needs protection from humans. It is the first vent animal declared endangered because scientists worry that the prospect of deep-sea mining, which may happen in the future, could threaten the snail's survival.

Sharing the snail's environment are crustaceans called Hoff crabs that have no eyes. They get their food from bacteria living in their chest hairs.

Vent creatures have special enzymes and proteins that enable them to survive in the scalding water, toxic fluids, and extreme pressure at the ocean's depths.

The Pompeii worm, named after the Italian city that was wiped out by a volcano in 79 AD, can withstand higher temperatures than almost any other animal—as high as 175 degrees F (79 degrees C). The hairy covering on its back, which is composed of colonies of bacteria, helps to insulate it from the heat. Large groups of these worms live on black smoker chimney walls in the Pacific Ocean.

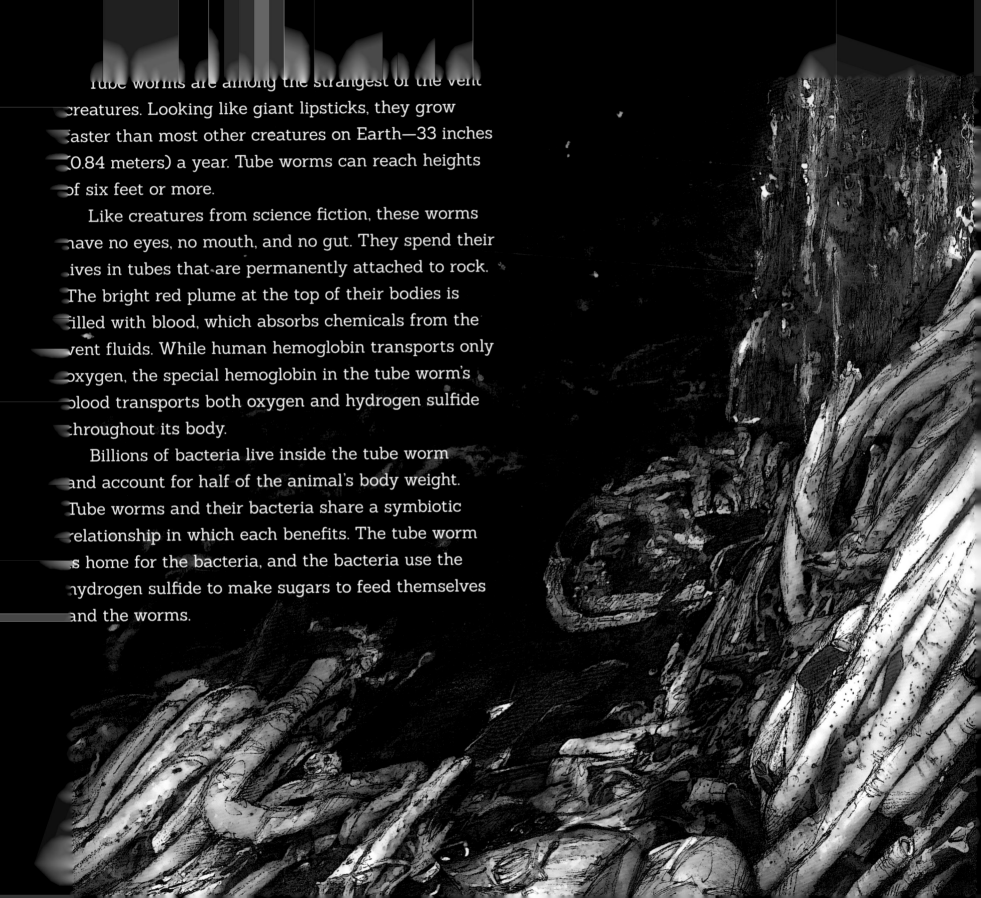

Tube worms are among the strangest of the vent creatures. Looking like giant lipsticks, they grow faster than most other creatures on Earth—33 inches (0.84 meters) a year. Tube worms can reach heights of six feet or more.

Like creatures from science fiction, these worms have no eyes, no mouth, and no gut. They spend their lives in tubes that are permanently attached to rock. The bright red plume at the top of their bodies is filled with blood, which absorbs chemicals from the vent fluids. While human hemoglobin transports only oxygen, the special hemoglobin in the tube worm's blood transports both oxygen and hydrogen sulfide throughout its body.

Billions of bacteria live inside the tube worm and account for half of the animal's body weight. Tube worms and their bacteria share a symbiotic relationship in which each benefits. The tube worm is home for the bacteria, and the bacteria use the hydrogen sulfide to make sugars to feed themselves and the worms.

Most animals that live
in the total darkness of the
vent ecosystem have evolved
so that they no longer have the
use of some sensory organs.

Blind shrimp have no eyes. Sight is
useless in a world without sunlight. But
these shrimp do have light-sensing organs on
their backs. Some researchers theorize that these
light sensors may be able to "see" an infrared glow
that is given off by hot vents.

These ghostly white, one-inch-long
(three-centimeters-long) shrimp have been found
three miles below the ocean's surface in the
Cayman Trough on the bottom of the western
Caribbean Sea—the deepest known hydrothermal
vent system. They feed on bacteria that they
cultivate on their bodies.

Unlike other octopuses, the vent octopus has few, if any, chromatophores—pigment cells that enable octopuses to change color. The pale, almost white, vent octopus cannot turn different colors or show patterns. It also lacks the ink sac that other octopuses use to cloak themselves and make a fast getaway from predators. In total darkness, color patterns and ink jets would not be seen.

Found only in Pacific Ocean vents, this octopus is small. Its head is no bigger than an adult's thumb.

Despite its size, the vent octopus is an aggressive predator, feeding on tiny crustaceans called amphipods. On one of her *Alvin* voyages to a vent site on the East Pacific Rise, American scientist Janet Voight discovered what she called a "feeding frenzy" of twelve octopuses that climbed onto a spire circling the vent and attacked a dense swarm of amphipods.

More than 650 vents are known, and new ones are continually being discovered around the world from the Arctic to Antarctica. To locate hydrothermal vents, scientists slowly tow a special instrument called a "Tow-yo" along the mid-ocean ridge at varying depths. The Tow-yo contains sensors that detect hot spots.

Researchers from many fields are studying deep ocean vents for potential uses. Some scientists are looking for medicines that might be made from vent organisms. One search has already led to the development of an antibiotic made from the Pompeii worm's bacteria. Another study of an enzyme from a vent microbe helped in the creation of a test for the coronavirus.

More than a dozen mining companies worldwide are trying to find out if it is possible to mine the seafloor for metals such as copper, zinc, lead, and gold flushed up from deep within Earth. But conservationists oppose seafloor mining because it could harm vent ecosystems.

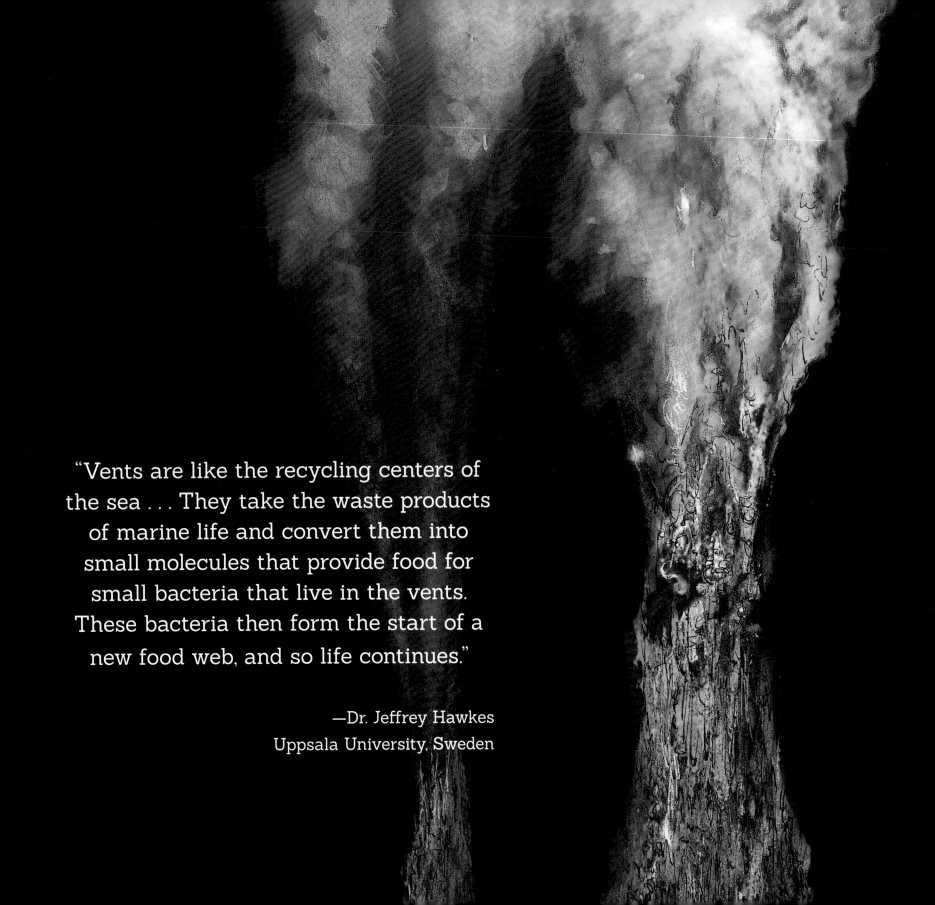

"Vents are like the recycling centers of
the sea . . . They take the waste products
of marine life and convert them into
small molecules that provide food for
small bacteria that live in the vents.
These bacteria then form the start of a
new food web, and so life continues."

—Dr. Jeffrey Hawkes
Uppsala University, Sweden

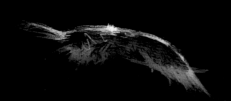

Discovery of hydrothermal vents revolutionized knowledge about Earth and the evolution of life. We now know that vents help to remove heat from Earth's interior and regulate ocean chemistry. Perhaps most amazing, we've learned that vents support life that depends on chemosynthesis powered by Earth rather than on photosynthesis powered by the sun.

Life on Earth may even have begun at vents. Single-celled microbes were the first forms of life—and the only living things for two billion years. Some scientists think these microbes appeared when conditions on the young planet were much like those in hydrothermal vents. Descendants of these microbes thrive in the extreme heat of vents today.

Along with tube worms, iron snails, and blind shrimp, Earth's great diversity of creatures is linked to the earliest chemistry of life.

These extreme environments at the bottom of the sea play an important part in the natural history of all life on Earth . . .

including our own.

LEARN MORE ABOUT THE DEEP OCEAN

1 Water covers 71 percent of Earth. Most of Earth's water (96.5 percent) is salt water in the oceans. Only 2.5 percent of Earth's water is fresh water that we can drink, and way more than half of that fresh water is trapped in ice and glaciers.

2 Sometimes undersea volcanic action breaks through the ocean's surface, creating islands such as Surtsey, which rose from the sea off Iceland during the early 1960s.

3 The mid-ocean ridge is the largest geological feature on Earth. It is a continuous range of volcanoes that wraps around the planet, stretching nearly 40,390 miles (65,000 kilometers). Ninety percent of the range lies in the deep ocean, more than 6,500 feet (2,000 meters) below the surface. The two most well studied mid-ocean ridges are the Mid-Atlantic Ridge and the East Pacific Rise.

4 Vent organisms are unique because they live in an environment that would be toxic to most other organisms on Earth.

5 The *Alvin* is one of very few human-operated deep-diving subs, also called human-operated vehicles (HOVs). *Alvin* is owned by the U.S. Navy and operated by Woods Hole Oceanographic Institution (WHOI). A few other countries, including China, France, Japan, and Russia, also have HOVs, and several are owned by private companies. *Alvin* was upgraded in 2021 to dive to 21,325 feet (6,500 meters).

6 Earth's surface is made up of gigantic pieces of crust and uppermost mantle called tectonic plates. The plates are continually moving at their boundaries, the places where they meet. Scientists recognize three types of plate movement: (1) convergent, where plates collide and raise mountains; (2) divergent, where two plates are moving away from each other, creating volcanoes, new seafloor and widening oceans; and (3) transform, where two plates slide horizontally past each other, creating a fault valley or undersea canyon and causing earthquakes.

7 Chemosynthesis supports many vent ecosystems, some of which have as much biomass (the total weight of organisms in a given area) as is found in tropical rain forests.

8 Even Antarctica's frigid waters have hydrothermal vents, in the Pacific-Antarctic Ridge.

9 The most well-studied mid-ocean ridges within the global system are the Mid-Atlantic Ridge and the East Pacific Rise. The Mid-Atlantic Ridge runs down the center of the Atlantic Ocean, slowly spreading apart at a rate of 0.8 to 2 inches (2 to 5 centimeters) per year. In contrast, the East Pacific Rise spreads quickly, at rates of around 2 to 6 inches (6 to 16 centimeters) per year.

10 Eighty percent of the world's volcanoes are underwater.

"The entire ocean volume circulates through hydrothermal vents every 40 million years."

—Dr. Jeffrey Hawkes, Uppsala University, Sweden

Author's Note

In 1870 French author Jules Verne published his science fiction novel, *Twenty Thousand Leagues Under the Sea*, in which he imagined a marvelous submarine, the *Nautilus*, which could enable its crew and the mysterious Captain Nemo to explore and even live in the hidden world beneath the ocean.

What Verne only imagined is now possible. No longer science fiction, deep-sea submersibles such as the *Alvin* take scientists to the bottom of the sea. In 1977, the discovery of hydrothermal vents and the community of vent creatures both surprised and amazed scientists. Famed American oceanographer Dr. Robert Ballard, who discovered where the sunken *Titanic* lay, was one of the first to see the vents. "Probably one of the biggest biological discoveries ever made on Earth," Ballard said of the find.*

Scientific discoveries that expand our knowledge and change the way we view the world are exciting. These are moments scientists live for, moments that demonstrate again and again that science is the best method we have for investigating the world and acquiring knowledge. It is science that liberated humans from the dark ages of superstition and ignorance by providing an objective method for obtaining evidence and using that as a basis for decisions that affect people's lives. Hydrothermal vents revealed a previously unknown life process—chemosynthesis—that depends on energy from Earth rather than from the sun. This amazing process may also have powered the evolution of life beyond Earth. Some scientists theorize that chemosynthesis might support life below the surface of Mars and on Jupiter's moon Europa. What we are learning about life in this otherworldly environment at the bottom of the sea may help us find life in other worlds in the extreme environment of space. And that's not science fiction!

* Bill Nye discusses discovery of hydrothermal vents with Dr. Robert Ballard
www.youtube.com/watch?v=D69hGvCsWgA

Glossary

chemosynthesis
the process that bacteria at hydrothermal vents use to convert chemicals from Earth into food for themselves and vent creatures

ecosystem
a community of organisms living in balance with each other and with their environment

geologist
a scientist who studies rocks to learn what Earth is made of and how it evolved

hemoglobin
protein in red blood cells that gives them their red color; hemoglobin transports oxygen to all the tissues of vertebrates (animals with backbones)

hydrothermal
hydro means water, and thermal means heat; hydrothermal refers to the action of heated water in Earth's crust

microbe
a microscopic organism such as a bacterium or a fungus

oceanographer
a scientist who studies the oceans

photosynthesis
the process that green plants and some other organisms use to turn water and carbon dioxide into food (sugar) using light energy from the sun

symbiosis
the living together of two or more different species of organisms

tectonic plate
a gigantic moving slab of Earth's solid outer layer, or surface. Powerful forces within Earth's mantle move these plates. There are seven major plates (the African, Antarctic, Eurasian, Indo-Australian, North American, Pacific, and South American) and many minor ones. Some plates, such as the African and South American Plates consist of both continents and oceans. The Pacific Plate, which is the largest, consists almost entirely of ocean.

Acknowledgments

Writing this book has been a vicarious journey to the amazing world of hydrothermal vents at the bottom of the sea. This journey would not have been possible without the help of scientists who have actually taken the plunge to hydrothermal vents, have seen them up close, and are expanding our knowledge of how processes deep within Earth have shaped and continue to shape our planet. I am profoundly grateful to the following people who generously shared their work with me, answered my questions by phone and/or email, and read portions or all of the manuscript: Dr. Edward T. Baker, Earth-Ocean Interactions, NOAA/Pacific Marine Environmental Laboratory; Dr. Chong Chen, Scientist with Tenure, Japan Agency for Marine-Earth Science and Technology (JAMSTEC), Yokosuka, Japan; Dr. Jeffrey Hawkes, Uppsala University, Sweden; Dr. Lauren S. Mullineaux, Senior Scientist and Chair, Biology Department, Woods Hole Oceanographic Institution; C. Nicolai Roterman, Associate Researcher, Department of Zoology, University of Oxford, John Krebs Field Station, Wytham, Oxford, UK; Dr. Janet Voight, Women's Board Associate Curator for Invertebrate Zoology, Negaunee Integrative Research Center, Field Museum, Chicago, Illinois.

Bringing a book from manuscript to publication takes a team, and I am fortunate to have had the opportunity to work with so many talented people. Special thanks to artist/illustrator Tom Gonzalez for creating the stunning images that bring my words to life. Huge thanks to Margaret Quinlin, Peachtree's publisher, for her continuing support of my work. Thanks to Adela Pons for the book's beautiful design and layout. Profound thanks to my editor Vicky Holifield, with whom I have had the privilege of working on five previous books. Vicky's insightful comments and constructive prodding always push my creativity and help to make each book the best it can be. Finally I thank Harvey Markowitz and my agent Barbara Markowitz for their long-time support and friendship.

Selected Bibliography

Books

Ballard, Robert, and Christopher Drew. *Into the Deep: A Memoir from the Man Who Found* Titanic. National Geographic, 2021.

Hague, Bradley. *Alien Deep: Revealing the Mysterious Living World at the Bottom of the Ocean*, National Geographic Children's Books, 2012.

Johnson, Rebecca L., *Journey into the Deep: Discovering New Ocean Creatures*. Millbrook Press, 2010.

Mallory, Kenneth, *Diving to a Deep-Sea Volcano* (Scientists in the Field Series). HMH Books for Young Readers, 2006.

Websites

National Oceanic and Atmospheric Administration (NOAA)
www.noaa.gov

Pacific Marine Environmental Laboratory
https://pmel.noaa.gov/

Woods Hole Oceanographic Institution (WHOI)
www.whoi.edu

Videos & Films

"Plate Tectonics."
An exploration of tectonic plates and Earth's constant transformation featuring oceanographer Dr. Robert Ballard.
National Geographic.
https://education.nationalgeographic.org/resource/plate-tectonics-video/

"The *Alvin*."
The deep-diving, human-operated vehicle (HOV), operated by Woods Hole Oceanographic Institution (WHOI), that takes scientists miles below the ocean's surface.
www.whoi.edu/what-we-do/explore/underwater-vehicles/hov-alvin/

"Deep Sea Hydrothermal Vents."
National Geographic short film.
www.nationalgeographic.org/media/deep-sea-hydrothermal-vents/

"Dive Deeper in *Alvin*."
A series of videos about *Alvin*.
https://vimeo.com/showcase/4261384

"Earth-Ocean Interactions." Pacific Marine Environmental Laboratory, National Oceanic and Atmospheric Administration (NOAA).
www.pmel.noaa.gov/eoi/

"Hydrothermal Vent Facts for Kids."
https://kids.kiddle.co/Hydrothermal_vent

"Hydrothermal Vents."
Bill Nye discusses the discovery of hydrothermal vents with Dr. Robert Ballard.
www.youtube.com/watch?v=D69hGvCsWgA

"Hydrothermal Vents."
Woods Hole Oceanographic Institution.
https://www.whoi.edu/multimedia/hydrothermal-vents